WHY

Grace

CHANGES
EVERYTHING

All Study material has been written by:
Jim and June Hesterly

Acts 1:8 Ministries, Inc.
P.O. Box 28771
Santa Ana, CA 92704

Study Guide

Published by Acts 1:8 Ministries, Inc.
P.O. Box 28771
Santa Ana, CA 92704

Library of Congress Catolging in Publication Data
Hesterly, James L.

ISBN 1-928779-02-6

This Study Guide has been designed to be used in conjunction with the book *Why Grace Changes Everything*, written by Pastor Chuck Smith. It can be used in small groups, classroom situations or personal studies. Each question can be answered by referring to the text *Why Grace Changes Everything* and by reading all scriptural references given.

All Study Guide material has been written by:

Jim & June Hesterly

Acts 1:8 Ministries, Inc.

P.O. Box 28771
Santa Ana, CA 92704
(714) 641-7132

TABLE OF CONTENTS

LESSON ONE

As you begin your study:

Always start with prayer, looking to the Lord for the Holy Spirit's guidance as you observe, interpret, and apply each lesson to your life.

1. Carefully read through "A Love Relationship with God" on page 7.

2. God has called us into a loving relationship with Himself. Our part is to _and _____.

3. What commandment did Jesus say was the greatest?

_____

_____

_____

4. Explain the *key* to our relationship with God and with one another.

_____

_____

_____

5. What sign indicates a fall into legalism?

_____

_____

_____

6. Describe God's intention for the law.

_____

_____

_____

7. How does the knowledge and experience of God's grace in our lives change everything?

_____

_____

LESSON TWO

1. Carefully read through Chapter 1, "Forgiven!", on page 17.

2. Explain why trying to become righteous only leads to failure.

_____

_____

_____

3. According to I John 1:8,10 how can we deceive ourselves?

_____

_____

_____

4. Explain our problem as stated in Romans 3:19,23.

_____

_____

_____

5. Describe God's view of our righteousness declared in Isaiah 64:6.

_____

_____

_____

6. Give a brief description of God's requirements for eternal life.

_____

_____

_____

7. What is God's standard of righteousness and how can we achieve it?

_____

_____

_____

8. What principle must be applied to enjoy fellowship with God?

_____

_____

_____

9. According to the New Testament, the word *grace* means

_____

_____

_____

10. Explain our basis for receiving God's grace and forgiveness into our lives.

_____

_____

_____

11. What results can we expect when we believe in the sacrifice that Jesus Christ made for us?

_____

_____

_____

12. Why is the gospel of grace the best news we will ever hear?

_____

_____

_____

LESSON THREE

1. Carefully read through Chapter 2, "The Door Is Never Closed", page 31.

2. By what means does God account us to be righteous?

_____

_____

_____

3. What is the problem in trying to establish righteousness by laws or by works?

_____

_____

_____

4. What are the two aspects of the gospel of grace?

   a. _____

      _____

   b. _____

      _____

5. In what ways does Satan challenge the good news of God's grace?

_____

_____

_____

_____

6. How should we respond to the accusations of Satan?

_____

_____

_____

7. Why is it folly to try to improve on the righteousness that God has imputed to those who believe?

_____

_____

_____

8. Explain the results of trying to relate to God on the basis of our own righteousness.

_____

_____

_____

9. Identify the *Siamese twins* of the New Testament and why they are always coupled together.

_____

_____

_____

10. Explain the meaning of the word *justified*.

_____

_____

_____

11. Because Jesus Christ is perfect, "I have His _____

credited to my account because of my _____

in Him".

LESSON FOUR

1. Carefully read through Chapter 3, "No Favorites in the Kingdom", page 45.

2. Give a brief description of the people God uses.

_____

_____

_____

3. Upon what basis does God choose the people He uses?

_____

_____

_____

4. Explain the beauty of the gospel as found in John 1:12.

_____

_____

_____

5. Briefly describe God's preparation of Paul for ministry.

_____

_____

_____

6. In what ways does God prepare each of us for ministry?

_____

_____

_____

7. For what purpose does God shape the events and circumstances of our lives?

_____

_____

8. Why is preparation so important to our fulfillment of the special work God has for each of us?

_____

_____

_____

9. In what ways does Satan try to discourage us?

_____

_____

_____

10. How can we overcome his condemnation?

_____

_____

_____

11. List the ways we can let Jesus shine forth:

a. _____

_____

b. _____

_____

c. _____

_____

d. _____

_____

1. Carefully read through Chapter 4, "A Portrait of Grace", page 63.

2. Briefly summarize the story of Abraham and his faith as told in Genesis 15.

_____

_____

_____

3. Why is Abraham called *the father of all those who believe*?

_____

_____

_____

4. Review Galations 4:22-31.

   a. What do Hagar and her son represent? _____

   _____

   b. What does Isaac represent? _____

   _____

5. Describe the blessings of those who seek right-standing with God through faith in Jesus Christ.

_____

_____

_____

6. At what moment does God credit righteousness to our account?

_____

_____

_____

7. What work does God require of us?

_____

_____

_____

8. How can we demonstrate our belief in God?

_____

_____

_____

9. Why must our actions be in harmony with what we believe?

_____

_____

_____

10. What results can we expect when we have true faith?

_____

_____

_____

11. How do we become *sons of Abraham*?

_____

_____

_____

12. Why is Abraham's life a *glorious picture* of what grace is and does?

_____

_____

_____

LESSON SIX

1. Carefully read through Chapter 5, "One Step at a Time", page 79.

2. Why is our relationship with Jesus Christ the foundation for everything that follows?

_____

_____

_____

3. How do we enjoy deep fellowship with God?

_____

_____

_____

4. Explain the meaning of the word *walk* in Galations 5:16.

_____

_____

_____

5. What does it mean to *walk in the Spirit*?

_____

_____

_____

6. How does our mind affect the decision to walk after the Spirit or to walk after our own fleshly desires?

_____

_____

_____

7. How can our lives begin to reflect the priorities of the Spirit?

_____

_____

_____

8. What is the solution for being set free from bondage to the flesh?

_____

_____

_____

9. In what ways can we *strengthen the Spirit* and walk in the Spirit?

_____

_____

10. Explain the necessity for feeding on God's word and communing with God through prayer.

_____

_____

11. What are some of the hindrances we face to having spiritual growth in our lives?

_____

_____

12. Explain the solution to these hindrances as given in Philippians 3:14 and Luke 13:24.

_____

_____

13. Describe the benefits we can expect as we walk in the Spirit.

_____

_____

LESSON SEVEN

1. Carefully read through Chapter 6, "A Garden, Not a Factory", page 95.

2. What comparison is Paul making in Galatians 3:2,3?

_____

_____

_____

3. What is the result of having a relationship with Christ?

_____

_____

_____

4. According to Matt. 7:20, how will we know *sheep* from *wolves*?

_____

_____

_____

5. What is God interested in and what does He look for in our lives?

_____

_____

_____

_____

6. How does the fruit of the Spirit blossom naturally from our lives?

_____

_____

_____

7. Describe the difference between *doing* and *being* and its relationship to bearing fruit.

_____

_____

_____

8. How can we please God?

_____

_____

_____

9. What takes place when we are filled with the love of God?

_____

_____

_____

10. Why is it impossible to improve on the righteousness given to us by God?

_____

_____

_____

11. Describe a relationship that is based on works.

_____

_____

_____

12. "The works of God are not wrought because of our righteousness.

They are wrought by_____."

1. Carefully read through Chapter 7, "Believing for the Blessings", page 111.

2. Give a brief explanation of Galatians 3:2.

_____

_____

_____

3. How does this verse relate to our receiving the indwelling, filling, and empowering of the Holy Spirit?

_____

_____

_____

4. How and why do we receive the blessings of God?

_____

_____

_____

5. Describe the spiritual warfare that we can expect when we ask God to fill us with His Holy Spirit.

_____

_____

_____

6. Why do so many Christians have problems in their Christian experience?

_____

_____

_____

7. In what way can II Chronicles 16:9 encourage those who have difficulty understanding God's blessings?

_____

_____

_____

8. List the three blessings promised to Abraham in the following verses:

   a. Genesis 15:1 _____

   b. Genesis 17:6 _____

   c. Genesis 17:7 _____

9. Why are these important to those who believe?

_____

_____

_____

10. What results can we expect when we simply believe God to keep His Word?

_____

_____

_____

LESSON NINE

1. Carefully read through Chapter 8, "The Struggle Begins", page 125.

2. Why do some believers never enjoy God's victory?

_____

_____

_____

3. Describe one of the greatest barriers to Christian growth and how we can find hope.

_____

_____

_____

4. Explain our cause for rejoicing in the fact that there is a real battle that exists.

_____

_____

_____

5. Describe the struggles that Peter and Paul experienced in their battles with their flesh:

   a. Peter: _____

   _____

   b. Paul: _____

   _____

6. Give a brief explanation of the problem described in Romans 7:21-23.

_____

_____

7. How can a God-given drive become a thing that wars against the Spirit?

_____

_____

_____

8. What provision has God made for our flesh?

_____

_____

_____

9. What biblical prescription has been given for resolving the conflict between the flesh and the Spirit? (Romans 6:6)

_____

_____

_____

10. What must we do with our specific areas of weakness?

_____

_____

_____

11. What results take place when we no longer live after the flesh but after the Spirit?

_____

_____

_____

LESSON TEN

1. Carefully read through Chapter 9, "Free Indeed!", page 141.

2. Give a brief explanation of the word *freedom* and what this word means to the believer.

_____

_____

_____

3. According to Ephesians 2:3, why were we all incapable of living right- eously?

_____

_____

_____

4. What must we do if we are to remain free in the liberty of Christ?

_____

_____

_____

5. How is Christian liberty sometimes perverted and how can we avoid this problem?

_____

_____

_____

6. In what way are we to use our Christian freedom?

_____

_____

_____

7. Why must we continually be on guard to maintain our freedom?

_____

_____

_____

8. What can we do to avoid things that would impede our progress as we "run the race that is set before us"?

_____

_____

_____

9. How can the application of I Corinthians 6:12 help us to maintain our freedom in Christ?

_____

_____

_____

LESSON ELEVEN

1. Carefully read through Chapter 10, "Won't They Go Wild?", page 153.

2. What important key do we have for our Christian walk?

_____

_____

_____

3. Why are we now free from the law, our sinful nature, and our guilt?

_____

_____

_____

_____

4. Why are we no longer living after the flesh?

_____

_____

_____

5. How can we deceive ourselves concerning the grace of God?

_____

_____

_____

6. In what ways can our lifestyle manifest the fact that we have been born of the Spirit?

_____

_____

_____

7. What results can we experience when we are tasting the goodness of God's love and loving Him in response?

_____

_____

_____

8. What is the *only true motivation for goodness*? _____

_____

_____

9. Why is II Corinthians 5:17 an *incredibly liberating truth*?

_____

_____

_____

10. What important distinction does Scripture make concerning our spirit and our body?_____

_____

_____

11. In our moments of weakness how can we experience victory?

_____

_____

12. Explain I John 5:3 and how we can choose to do what is right and to refrain from evil._____

_____

13. Why is our relationship with God steady and secure?

_____

_____

_____

LESSON TWELVE

1. Carefully read through Chapter 11, "Booby Traps and Land Mines", page 169.

2. In what ways do cults tend to pervert the gospel of Christ?

_____

_____

_____

3. Give a brief explanation of Galatians 1:8 and the word *anathema*.

_____

_____

_____

4. Why was Paul so adamant in his statement to the Galatian church?

_____

_____

_____

5. Describe the frequently used tactics of false teachers that are used to make new converts.

_____

_____

_____

6. What sad results can be expected when we buy into false teaching?

_____

_____

_____

7. What is the best safeguard against this kind of deception?

_____

_____

_____

8.Why does the message of legalism tend only to alienate us from the work God has done in our hearts through faith in Jesus Christ?

_____

_____

_____

9. How can we have a beautiful, unbroken relationship with God?

_____

_____

_____

LESSON THIRTEEN

1. Carefully read through Chapter 12, "All or Nothing", page 183.

2. Why is it crucial that we stand fast on the truth of God's Word?

_____

_____

_____

3. How does God's Word bring stability to our lives?

_____

_____

_____

4. In what way is Paul's exhortation in Galatian 5:1 relevant for us today?

_____

_____

_____

5. Describe some of the earmarks of *bondage-based* groups.

_____

_____

_____

6. Briefly explain Paul's admonition given in Galatians 5:2.

_____

_____

_____

_____

7. What is the logical result of looking to the law for righteousness?

8. Our righteousness is a result of _____

_____

_____

_____

9. What crucial choice has been set before us?

_____

_____

_____

10. How are we able to *stand in grace*?

_____

_____

_____

LESSON FOURTEEN

1. Carefully read through Chapter 13, "Members of Royalty", page 199.

2. Briefly explain Paul's illustration of the life situation of an heir as given in Galatians 4:1,2.

_____

_____

_____

3. In what way does this illustrate the relationship of the law to God's people?

_____

_____

_____

4. What results can we expect if we are living by the law?

_____

_____

_____

5. Give a brief explanation of the legal procedures governing the granting of an inheritance.

_____

_____

_____

6. Why is this important when we consider the *fullness of time*?

_____

_____

_____

7.What was Paul implying when he spoke of Christ being *sent* by the
Father?

_____

_____

_____

8.How can we enter into a wonderful, intimate relationship with God?

_____

_____

_____

9. Describe the relationship that God desires each of us to experience with
Him as our Father.

_____

_____

_____

10. How can we become heirs of God?

_____

_____

_____

11. What are some of the elements of our inheritance that are ours because
we have been made *joint heirs* with Jesus?

_____

_____

_____

LESSON FIFTEEN

1. Carefully read through Chapter 14, "Our Sole Responsibility", page 213.

2. What is the simple message of the New Testament?

   _____

   _____

   _____

3. Righteousness must either come by _____

   or by a perfect keeping of_____."

4. What results can be expected if we seek to be righteous before God by our works?

   _____

   _____

   _____

5. Why is justification by good works impossible?

   _____

   _____

   _____

6. How then, can we be justified?

   _____

   _____

   _____

7. What message is highlighted by the New Testament?

   _____

   _____

   _____

8. What is the one simple responsibility that we have been given by God?

_____

_____

_____

9. How is the righteousness of Jesus imparted to us?

_____

_____

_____

10. How will you respond to God's gracious provision?

_____

_____

_____